W9-AEC-432

ONE-ACT PLAYS

FOR

STAGE AND STUDY

Fifth Series

ONE-ACT PLAYS
FOR STAGE AND STUDY
First Series
PREFACE BY AUGUSTUS THOMAS

Twenty-five Contemporary Plays by American, English
and Irish Dramatists

IN ONE BOUND VOLUME   PRICE $3.00

ONE-ACT PLAYS
FOR STAGE AND STUDY
Second Series
PREFACE BY
WALTER PRICHARD EATON

Twenty-one Contemporary Plays, never before published
in book form, by American, English, Irish, French
and Hungarian Dramatists

IN ONE BOUND VOLUME   PRICE $3.00

ONE-ACT PLAYS
FOR STAGE AND STUDY
Third Series
PREFACE BY PERCIVAL WILDE

Twenty-one Contemporary Plays, never before published
in book form, by American, English and Irish
Dramatists

IN ONE BOUND VOLUME   PRICE $3.00

ONE-ACT PLAYS
FOR STAGE AND STUDY
Fourth Series
PREFACE BY PAUL GREEN

Twenty-one Contemporary Plays, never before published
in book form, by American, English and Irish
Dramatists

IN ONE BOUND VOLUME   PRICE $3.00

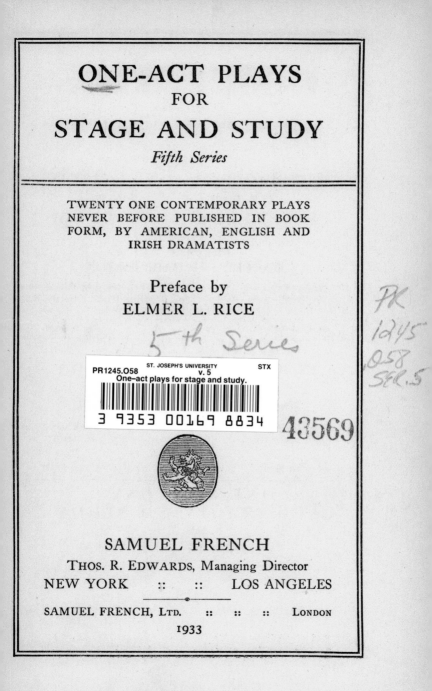

ONE-ACT PLAYS
FOR
STAGE AND STUDY
Fifth Series

TWENTY ONE CONTEMPORARY PLAYS
NEVER BEFORE PUBLISHED IN BOOK
FORM, BY AMERICAN, ENGLISH AND
IRISH DRAMATISTS

Preface by
ELMER L. RICE

5 th Series

PR1245.O58

ST. JOSEPH'S UNIVERSITY
v. 5
One-act plays for stage and study.

STX

3 9353 00169 8834

43569

PK 1245 .O58 SER.5

SAMUEL FRENCH
THOS. R. EDWARDS, Managing Director
NEW YORK :: :: LOS ANGELES

SAMUEL FRENCH, LTD. :: :: :: LONDON
1933

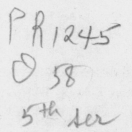

Copyright, 1929, by Samuel French

*All the plays in this book are printed through the courtesy of and
by special arrangement with the authors or their representatives.
The acting rights, whether professional or amateur, are in
every case fully protected by law. Application for the
right of performing any of the plays included in this
volume must be made to Samuel French, 25
West 45th Street, New York City.*

MANUFACTURED IN THE UNITED STATES OF AMERICA
BY THE VAIL-BALLOU PRESS, INC., BINGHAMTON, N. Y.

CONTENTS

PREFACE

BY ELMER RICE

It is easy to make out an excellent theoretical case against the merits of the one-act play, as a literary form. As with the short-story, the arbitrary limitation of time and space imposes upon the writer the necessity of stripping his material to its barest essentials in order to accommodate it to the narrow confines of the chosen form. It is a little like those puzzles in which one is required to fit together a number of fragments of irregular shape in such a way that a perfect square is formed. The game consists in fitting the pieces together; and the fact that, in itself, a perfect square is not especially interesting is irrelevant.

In other words, the exigencies of the one-act play tend to throw the emphasis upon form rather than upon substance. Technical skill counts for more than the poetic gift; and inventive ingenuity is more telling than the free flowering of inspiration. What is likely to result is a *tour de force*: a pretty mechanical contrivance which, however much it may excite our admiration, is scarcely calculated to induce that emotional catharsis which is presumably the chief function (or, let us say, effect) of art at its best.

We are all familiar with the devitalized O. Henry formula: a more or less cunningly contrived series of incidents culminating in a fore-ordained "tag": a mild fillip to the senses of the not too-exacting reader—the kind of expectedly unexpected shock which one receives, upon grasping the handles of an electric-vibration machine, or upon taking the sudden but awaited dips on a roller-coaster. This device, which seemed so charming only a little while ago, strikes us now as a childish and rather cheap, journalistic trick. It is the sort of thing that anybody can do with a silk hat, a large handkerchief and moderately deft fingers.

The one-act play tends to exhibit the same characteristics. There is no space for exposition, for the elaborate development of character, or for those apparently superficial adornments which actually give a hint to what lies within. Instead of an organic growth, we see a piece of carpentry: more often than not an expanded anecdote, the "point" of which is its last line or final situation. At its crudest, this type of drama is represented by the "black-out" sketches, familiar to the assiduous frequenter of revues; its more refined state we discover in such a confection as J. M. Barrie's Half-an-Hour. The difference between this and drama at its best, is the difference between journalism and literature, between illustration and painting, between "program" music and "pure" music. It may be art, but it is art at a low level.

Having taken what I regard as a very good hypothetical position with relation to the one-act play, I am now compelled to make the embarrassing confession that my hypothesis (like so many excellent hypotheses) does not match the facts.

For an examination of modern dramatic literature soon discloses the disconcerting truth that some of its finest products are one-act plays. There is no greater modern play in the English language than Synge's Riders to the Sea. Indeed, I know of no English play since Shakespeare that can match it. Shaw's best work, in my opinion, is The Showing Up of Blanco Posnet. Schnitzler has reached a high level of comedy in the Anatol sketches and of romantic melodrama in The Green Cockatoo. Some of Lord Dunsany's early fantasies are delightful compounds of exotic charm and poetic fancy. Edna St. Vincent Millay's Aria de Capo is, to the best of my knowledge, the only actable poetic play that has been written in America. Eugene O'Neill's one-act plays number among them some of his finest achievements (notably Ile, Bound East for Cardiff and the first act of Anna Christie, which is really a one-act play). J. M. Barrie is at his best in his one-act plays (although this, I think, is because a little of Barrie is likely to be better than a great deal). Dreiser's Plays of the Natural and Supernatural include some enormously interesting experiments—the fore-runners of expressionism. Porto-Riche's Francoise's Luck is altogether charming. Strindberg, Chekov, Andreyev, Lady Gregory, and Yeats have all written one-act plays of more than ordinary merit.

Apparently then, I have adduced enough evidence to demolish completely my own excellent argument. But I cannot allow myself to be so easily discredited (even by myself) and so I rush to my own defense with a plea of extenuating circumstances. For, if the reader will take the trouble to analyze the works I have enumerated, he will find that most of them are, in fact, *tours de force;* that concealed beneath the poetry, the art and all the graces, is the gaunt skeleton of the "black-out" sketch: the neat precision of the anecdote, the inevitable scoring of points or completion of a circuit. So that the fact that great dramatists have written great one-act plays does not argue the merits of the form, but merely demonstrates that a supreme artist can, upon occasion, break down the limitations of a given form and shape it to his will. George Borrow managed to make readable an account of the distribution of Bibles; and I think that a filling-station, designed by Michael Angelo and painted by Cezanne would be worth looking at. For artists of the first rank, rules do not exist.

One-act plays are more likely to be interesting in the study than in the theatre. An audience seems to demand an accumulation of emotion which the brief traffic of the one-act play does not permit. The characters are whisked away almost before one has had an opportunity to make their acquaintance. And to meet, in an evening, three or four alien groups of people, in as many diverse settings, is a little disconcerting and more than a little fatiguing. But, perhaps, that is merely an idiosyncrasy of my own. For it occurs to me that I always find the theatre more than a little fatiguing.

A DIADEM OF SNOW

A Play in One Act

BY

ELMER RICE

ELMER RICE

Elmer Rice was born in New York City in 1892. He is a self-confessed New Yorker, one of the few successful playwrights about whom this can be justly said. He was graduated with high honors from the New York Law School. His first play was *On Trial*, which was produced in 1914. He was for a time associated with the Morningside Players and other amateur organizations. For some years after the production of *On Trial*, he wrote plays either alone or in collaboration. In 1921, together with Hatcher Hughes, he wrote *Wake Up, Jonathan*, which was produced by Mrs. Fiske. In 1923 came one of his best known successes, *The Adding Machine*, which has been acted in England and several countries on the Continent, as well as by the Theater Guild in New York. In 1924, he wrote, with Dorothy Parker, *Close Harmony*, which successfully toured on the road under the title of *The Lady Next Door*. Then, with Philip Barry, he wrote *Cock Robin*, a successful mystery play produced in 1927. His next was *Street Scene*, one of the outstanding successes of the present season, and winner of the Pulitzer Prize for 1929. His latest play, *See Naples and Die*, is now having a successful New York run.

Published Plays: *On Trial; The Adding Machine; Close Harmony* (with Dorothy Parker); *Wake up Jonathan* (with Hatcher Hughes); *Cock Robin* (with Philip Barry); *The Subway; The Passing of Chow Chow; The Home of the Free; Street Scene; A Diadem of Snow.*

CHARACTERS

NICHOLAS ROMANOFF

MRS. ROMANOFF

ALIOSHA

THE ENVOY

MRS. OSHINSKY

The scene is laid in Tobolsk, Siberia. The time is November, 1917.

ALL RIGHTS RESERVED

A Diadem of Snow is copyright, 1917, by the Author, and 1929, by Samuel French, and is subject to a royalty. All acting rights, professional and amateur, broadcasting by radio, public reading, recitation, etc., are reserved in the United States of America, the British Empire, including the Dominion of Canada, and the other countries of the Copyright Union, by the owner. Performance forbidden and right of presentation reserved. Application for the right of performing this play must be made to Samuel French, 25 West 45th St., New York City, N. Y.

A DIADEM OF SNOW

A room furnished in execrable taste. To be sure, the table, the several chairs, the sideboard, and so forth all belong to the genus furniture [just as both Mr. LaFollette and Mr. Elihu Root belong to the Republican Party] but there the kinship ends. It is apparent that we are confronted with the handiwork of the Russian representative of some American easy-payment home-furnishing company. The only object in the room which does not merit instant annihilation is a much-battered samovar, which seems to be seeking in its memories of better days, a refuge from its present associates. On the walls are several framed placards, bearing in multi-colored Russian characters the legends: "Home, Sweet Home!", "Try, Try Again," "Life is Real, Life is Earnest," and other sentiments of like import. But the most conspicuous object on the walls is a wretchedly executed crayon enlargement of a man's photograph. It is hideously framed in gilt and profusely draped with black crêpe. The face, from the snaky hair to the long, straggly beard, is unbelievably vicious. The more erudite among the audience immediately recognize the beloved features of the late lamented Grigory Rasputin, but to the million it is just a bad picture of an ugly man.

There are windows in the rear wall, a door in the left wall and two doors in the right wall. It is evening in late November and dusk has already fallen. On the table is a large kerosene lamp, already lighted. The table is set for three.

A moment after the rise of the curtain, someone knocks sharply on the door at the left. Obtaining no response, the person knocks again. There is another brief pause, then the door opens and an untidy woman, wearing an apron over a wrapper, enters.

THE WOMAN [*calling to someone outside*]. Come right in, grand-daddy! I guess she's in the kitchen gettin' supper ready. She always leaves everything till the last minute.

[*A* MAN *enters. He is, apparently, in the last stages of decrepitude. He has a flowing white beard, flowing white hair and enormous smoked spectacles. He wears a huge over-coat and leans heavily on a stout cane.*]

THE MAN. [*in a feeble voice*]. A thousand thanks.

THE WOMAN. Sit down! I'll call her for you. You don't seem to have any too much voice of your own.

THE MAN. You are very good.

THE WOMAN [*calling*]. Mrs. Romanoff! Oh! Mrs. Romanoff!

A SHRILL VOICE [*from the right*]. Vell?

THE WOMAN [*in sing-song tones*]. This is Mrs. Oshinsky! There's an old man here to see you!

THE VOICE [*irritably*]. Vell, all right! He should vait! [*The speaker has a marked German accent.*]

MRS. OSHINSKY. She says you should wait.

THE MAN. Thank you.

MRS. OSHINSKY [*eyeing him curiously*]. If you've come to col-lect on the furniture, I might as well tell you, you won't get a kopeck. All the money her old man brings in—and Gawd knows it ain't much!—goes into prayers for *him!* [*She points a finger of scorn at poor Rasputin. The man involuntarily raises his head.*] And she a married woman! If it was me, my Petroushka would give me a crack over the head, that's what he would give me. But her man! [*She snorts with con-tempt.*] He lets her walk all over him. [*Her curiosity gain-ing the ascendancy again.*] Did you say you was from the baker's? [*Sharply, as he does not reply.*] Say, you ain't deef, too, are you?

[*One of the doors at the right opens and* MRS. ROMANOFF *enters. She wears an all-encompassing gingham bungalow apron. Her hair is in disorder and she wipes her red face with the back of her hand.*]

MRS. ROMANOFF [*sharply to the man*]. Vell, vot do you want?

MRS. OSHINSKY. He's hard of hearin'. He knocked at my door

by mistake. I told him that if he was after money, he might save himself climbin' the stairs, but he—

MRS. ROMANOFF [*sweetly*]. Dot's very kind of you, Mrs. Oshinsky. I'm not surprised dot you took him for a bill collector, I guess dot's all vat efer knocks at your door.

MRS. OSHINSKY. Well, at least, they never find me on my knees, sayin' prayers for a rotten—

MRS. ROMANOFF [*white with rage*]. Get out of my house!

MRS. OSHINSKY. Who wants to stay in your house? It ain't no place for a decent woman! [*She makes a long nose at the unoffending Rasputin and goes out.* MRS. ROMANOFF, *inarticulate with rage, stamps her foot violently.*]

MRS. ROMANOFF [*recovering speech*]. Vell, who are you and vat do you want? [*Before the man can reply.*] I've got no money for charidy! Go to the semstvo. They give money away like vater. Everybody with a pain in his little finger can get five rubles—ten rubles—fifty rubles. A fine country—

THE MAN [*in a whisper*]. Are we alone?

MRS. ROMANOFF [*in astonishment*]. Are you drunk or vat?

THE MAN [*mysteriously*]. Sh! [*He tip-toes to the windows and pulls down the shades.*]

MRS. ROMANOFF [*shrilly*]. Are you crazy?

[*The man, without a word, removes his overcoat and sheds his wig, his whiskers and his goggles, revealing the dapper figure and amiable features so dear to every American.*]

MRS. ROMANOFF [*in utter bewilderment*]. Von Bernstorff!

BERNSTORFF [*kissing her hand*]. Your royal highness!

MRS. ROMANOFF. Aber, es ist nicht möglich. How come you here to Tobolsk?

BERNSTORFF. I have come from Berlin, expressly to see your majesty.

MRS. ROMANOFF [*with a sigh*]. Ah, Berlin! Berlin! Ven shall I see you again! [*She wipes her eyes.*]

BERNSTORFF. I am overjoyed to find your majesty in good health. I was profoundly—

MRS. ROMANOFF [*coming out of her reverie*]. But, Bernstorff! It is not safe for you to be here!

BERNSTORFF [*with a smile*]. My disguise has allayed all suspicion.

MRS. ROMANOFF [*nervously*]. But if you should be found here—

BERNSTORFF. I am prepared for every emergency. [*He draws a book from his right-hand coat pocket.*] A book by Liebknecht! [*He draws a book from his left-hand coat pocket.*] A book by Maximilian Harden! [*With a wink.*] I am a Social-Democrat seeking refuge in free Russia. Ah, your majesty, a member of the Imperial Diplomatic Corps is equal to anything.

MRS. ROMANOFF [*still worried*]. It is a great danger—

BERNSTORFF. Danger! What is danger to me! To me who have come out of America alive! But do not alarm yourself, your majesty. I have travelled unmolested from the German frontier. No one has detained me, not one has questioned me. If there were any spies following me—

MRS. ROMANOFF. There are no more spies in Russia.

BERNSTORFF [*in utter amazement*]. No more spies! Have they gone mad, your Russians? Do they think, then, that freedom means that one can do whatever one likes?

MRS. ROMANOFF. Yes! Think of it, Bernstorff, to do whatever one likes! Even I—an empress!—they force me to do whatever I like! It is a terrible responsibility—a terrible responsibility. You, who have only to obey, cannot realize it. Ach! It makes my head to schwim!

BERNSTORFF. Ah, your majesty, I cannot find words to express my grief at seeing you like this—in these hideous surroundings.

MRS. ROMANOFF [*bristling*]. Hideous? Why are they hideous?

BERNSTORFF [*taken aback*]. But, surely—

MRS. ROMANOFF [*huffily*]. You do not like our furnishings? Vell, that is a matter of taste. They please us—Nicholas and I.

BERNSTORFF. A thousand pardons. I was—

MRS. ROMANOFF. You think because this room is not furnished in the manner of the Imperial Palace in Berlin, that we must be miserable here? Vell, you are wrong. All my life I have lived in great, gloomy rooms—in my father's palace in Hesse, in that terrible Winter Palace in Petrograd, in Moscow, in Tsarskoe-Selo. Always other people have chosen the bed I slept in, the table I ate from, the carpet I walked on—everything! My very tooth-brush even! Always other people! Here, at least, we have chosen things to please ourselves. Perhaps to you they are not beautiful, but to us they make a home! [*Laying her hand solemnly on* BERNSTORFF's *arm.*] The first home, Bernstorff, that we have ever had!

BERNSTORFF [*utterly amazed*]. But—but surely, your majesty, you are not happy here! Only a moment ago, I heard you subjected to unbelievable insults by a common woman! If I had dared—

MRS. ROMANOFF [*interrupting*]. Ah! You mean Mrs. Oshinsky! A harmless, lazy busy-body. In the Winter Palace, Bernstorff, there were five hundred busy-bodies—only they were not harmless. Here, I can tell my friend from my enemy. I know who—[*A great spluttering is heard from the room at the right.*] Gott in Himmel! Meine linsen suppe! [*She rushes out of the room.* BERNSTORFF, *sits with knitted brows, his growing bewilderment plainly shown on his face.*]

MRS. ROMANOFF [*re-entering*]. Ruined! My beautiful lentil soup is ruined! That comes of sitting here and schnattering!

BERNSTORFF [*explosively*]. It is not possible that these—these menial domestic duties—cooking—and—and—are performed by your majesty!

MRS. ROMANOFF [*looking at him in surprise*]. Who should do it then? The girls are all in Petrograd, studying—what do you call it?—type-setting and dressmaking and—God knows what!

BERNSTORFF [*almost inarticulate*]. But your servants! Where are your servants? Is it possible that this rabble that calls itself a government does not supply you with the means to retain servants?

MRS. ROMANOFF [*smiling*]. Do you think Nicholas would permit me to keep a servant?

BERNSTORFF [*utterly incredulous*]. You mean his majesty—! [*He stops on the very verge of apoplexy.*]

MRS. ROMANOFF. Among freemen, he says, there are no servants.

BERNSTORFF. I do not understand! In America, they talk much about democracy, but this—!

MRS. ROMANOFF. I do not understand either. I do not understand the Russian people. I have lived many years among them, but I do not understand them. [*Solemnly.*] They are not like the Germans, Bernstorff.

BERNSTORFF. No! [*Shaking his head.*] God pity them!

MRS. ROMANOFF. I do not understand Nicholas, either. With him, too, I have lived many years, but I do not understand him. Do you know, Bernstorff, he is beginning to read! At his age, he is beginning to read books—not holy books, mark you—but—[*Her voice drops to a whisper.*] Tolstoi—and Kropotkin—and Maxim Gorki! [*A neighboring clock strikes six.*] Six o'clock! He will be home soon. [*She begins removing her apron.*]

BERNSTORFF. All this that you have told me—[*He notices suddenly that she is clad in deep mourning and becomes greatly alarmed.*] You are in mourning! Has there been a bereavement? The Czarevitch—! [*He stops in dismay.*]

MRS. ROMANOFF. No, no! My Aliosha is well, Gott sei dank!

BERNSTORFF [*greatly relieved*]. Not one of the royal princesses, I hope.

MRS. ROMANOFF. No, it is for my Rasputin! For Grigory! [*She points to the picture.*] My poor Grigory!

BERNSTORFF. Ah yes! A very clever man!

MRS. ROMANOFF [*weeping silently*]. A saint, Bernstorff, a saint!

BERNSTORFF. Undoubtedly! If he were still alive—

MRS. ROMANOFF. No, no! He is happy, up there among the angels! He is freed from a world too base to understand him. [*She weeps copiously.*]

BERNSTORFF. From a strictly religious viewpoint, no doubt, there are, as your majesty suggests, compensations for his untimely end. But nevertheless, it is to be regretted that at this juncture his political genius—

MRS. ROMANOFF [*sadly reproachful*]. Ach, Bernstorff, Bernstorff, how can you talk of politics and of that holy man in one breath? It is desecration!

BERNSTORFF. I must respectfully disagree with your majesty. My imperial master has invested welt-politik with the sacredness of religion. The operations of the Imperial German Government are political manifestations of the will of God. And it is a sacred political mission that brings me here.

MRS. ROMANOFF [*mildly surprised*]. You come to Siberia— to Tobolsk—on political business?

BERNSTORFF [*nodding gravely*]. On political business of the most vital concern to your majesty.

MRS. ROMANOFF [*shaking her head*]. No, no! I have no interest in politics. I never understood them and I never shall. I have time only for my cooking and my prayers.

BERNSTORFF. When your majesty hears the nature of my errand—

MRS. ROMANOFF. It does not matter! For Grigory's sake, I tried to understand all that buzz-buzz-buzz at the Winter Palace,—but now Grigory is among the holy saints and I— [*She breaks off, wiping her eyes.*]

BERNSTORFF [*with great deliberation*]. Your majesty, I have come to restore Emperor Nicholas II. to his throne!

MRS. ROMANOFF [*with a startled cry*]. Ach Gott! Vat are you saying!

BERNSTORFF [*nodding solemnly*]. Yes!

MRS. ROMANOFF. But—but it is not possible!

BERNSTORFF [*drawing himself up, proudly*]. To the Imperial German Government, all things are possible!

MRS. ROMANOFF. But how—? [*She stops in bewilderment.*]

BERNSTORFF [*smiling*]. Your majesty need not concern herself with the modus operandi. The best brains in the German Foreign Office—that is to say the best brains in the world—

have applied themselves to the organization of the machin-ery which will accomplish the restoration. All that it is neces-sary for your majesty to do is to place implicit trust in me. Could anything be easier?

MRS. ROMANOFF [*half to herself*]. To go back there—back to Petrograd—back to the Winter Palace—back to—[*She covers her eyes and shudders.*]

BERNSTORFF. Your majesty—

MRS. ROMANOFF [*not heeding him*]. I thought I was free! I thought—I thought—[*She looks up suddenly at Rasputin's picture.*] Yes, Grigory! Yes, my saint! It is the will of God! I will do it!

BERNSTORFF [*with a cry of relief*]. Ah! I know your maj-esty—!

MRS. ROMANOFF [*as before*]. I will do it! For Aliosha's sake! For my Aliosha. It is his birthright! He was born to rule, Grigory said. And he shall rule! He shall rule! [*She falls into an ecstatic silence, her hands clasped, her eyes raised. Suddenly the tramping of heavy boots and the sound of a man whistling "Poor Butterfly" out of key, is heard at the left.*]

BERNSTORFF [*in alarm*]. Is someone coming?

MRS. ROMANOFF [*restored to herself*]. Ach Gott! Der Nicho-las! I had forgotten all about him. He must not find you here, Bernstorff! I must prepare him. Go quickly to the kitchen there.

BERNSTORFF. You will point out to him—

MRS. ROMANOFF. Yes, yes! Quick, he is coming! Do not come until I call you!

[BERNSTORFF *goes hastily into the kitchen, taking with him the appurtenances of his disguise, but leaving behind the two books.* MRS. ROMANOFF *busies herself at the table. The door at the left opens and* NICHOLAS ROMANOFF, *erstwhile Czar of all the Russias, enters. He wears a fur cap, a heavy overcoat with a fur collar, thick gloves and high rubber boots. He carries a large wooden snow-shovel. His cheeks are bright with health and his shoulders are broad and straight.*]

ROMANOFF [*kissing his wife*]. Well, old lady! Another day's work done! [*He removes his gloves.*]

MRS. ROMANOFF [*nervously*]. You are late.

ROMANOFF. Do not scold me for that. I stopped at Petkoff's shop.

MRS. ROMANOFF. Why did you do that? We have already too much food in the house.

ROMANOFF. But wait until you see what I have brought! [*He fishes in his coat pocket and produces a paper package.*] Some young onions! [*He fishes in the other pocket.*] And a pickled herring! Tcha! the juice has run! That Petkoff is not liberal with his paper! [*He licks his finger.*] Ah! Excellent! This will go nicely with your lentil soup, little mother. [*He removes his cap and overcoat, talking all the while. He wears a long workingman's blouse.*] If I were to describe to you my appetite, you would not believe me. Hard work! That is the best sauce! Do you know what I said to Gobloff, the foreman? "Gobloff," I said, "every shovelful of snow in the cart is a spoonful of lentil soup in my belly."

MRS. ROMANOFF [*sharply*]. There will be no lentil soup in your belly tonight!

ROMANOFF [*his face falling*]. What do you say? No lentil soup?

MRS. ROMANOFF. The soup is spoiled.

ROMANOFF [*swallowing a lump*]. Spoiled! [*With a great effort he recovers his cheerfulness.*] Well, well! That can happen, too! [*Patting her shoulder.*] Come, come, little mother, the world cannot stop because our lentil soup is spoiled! [*Very solemnly.*] It is God's punishment for my greediness! [*He seats himself and begins removing his boots.* MRS. ROMANOFF *watches him nervously, not knowing how to divulge the disturbing news.*]

ROMANOFF [*looking up*]. Where is Aliosha?

MRS. ROMANOFF [*relieved by the interruption*]. He is on the street playing with the boys. [*She goes to the window, worried.*] He should not be out after dark. [*She peers anxiously out of the window.*]

ROMANOFF. He is a good boy. No harm will come to him. [*In his stocking feet, he goes toward the kitchen door. As he nears the door,* MRS. ROMANOFF *turns and sees him. She utters an exclamation of alarm.*]

MRS. ROMANOFF. Nicky! Vere are you going?

ROMANOFF [*apologetically*]. I was going for my slippers. I thought I should find them, in their accustomed place, by the kitchen stove.

MRS. ROMANOFF. Yes, yes! They are there! But I shall get them for you.

ROMANOFF. No, no! I must fetch my own slippers. [*He makes a movement toward the door.*]

MRS. ROMANOFF [*sharply*]. Are you verrückt? To walk in your stocking feet around! Do you want to get a splinter? You stay right here! [*She goes hastily into the kitchen.*]

ROMANOFF. You think of everything, little mother! [*He walks toward the table, picks up one of the empty soup plates and shakes his head sorrowfully.*] Spoiled! Well, well! [*He puts down the plate with a sigh.* MRS. ROMANOFF *enters with the slippers.*]

MRS. ROMANOFF. Here are the slippers!

ROMANOFF. You are a saint, little mother! [*He puts on the slippers with a sigh of satisfaction.*] Ah! That's fine! As warm as toast! The snow is very cold! But it is a good cold —a dry cold! It is not like the cold of the dungeons in the Fortress of St. Peter and St. Paul. I must read to you Kropotkin's description—

MRS. ROMANOFF. Nicky, I have something to tell you—

ROMANOFF. Not now! An empty stomach is a bad listener. Wait until my belt is tight. Then you can tell me what Mrs. Oshinsky said to you and what you replied to her—

MRS. ROMANOFF. It has nothing to do with Mrs. Oshinsky.

ROMANOFF. Well, well, whatever it is, it will not spoil. Where is Aliosha? We must hasten. Tonight we are all going to the Trotsky Theatre. If we do not arrive early, all the seats will be taken.

MRS. ROMANOFF [*firmly*]. We cannot go tonight!

ROMANOFF [*protesting*]. But we must! They are showing Charlie Chaplin in "Laughing Gas." It is the last night! Everyone is talking about it! Kanowsky, the cart-driver, swears that he laughed until the tears ran. He is not lying. You can see the streaks on his face. And Gobloff! Do you know what Gobloff told me? [*Impressively.*] He went last night with his family and his wife's mother—Marya Petrovna—actually burst a blood-vessel laughing! [*Solemnly.*] They had to send for a doctor!

MRS. ROMANOFF. Nicky, it is no time for foolishness! It is no time for eating! There is something—something—

ROMANOFF [*impressed by her solemnity*]. What is it, little mother? Have you had a vision?

MRS. ROMANOFF [*nervously*]. Yes! A vision!

ROMANOFF [*excitedly*]. A saint has appeared to you? A holy saint?

MRS. ROMANOFF [*shaking her head*]. No, not a saint, exactly. Listen, Nicky—

ROMANOFF. Not a saint? An angel, then?

MRS. ROMANOFF [*impatiently*]. No, not an angel! [*Sharply*]. Be still and listen—

[*A scuffling and a confusion of voices is heard outside the entrance-door.*]

MRS. ROMANOFF [*alarmed*]. Aliosha! [*She hurries to the door and opens it.* MRS. OSHINSKY *enters dragging* ALIOSHA *by the collar. The boy's face is streaked with dirt and tears, his clothes are in disorder and his stockings are full of holes.*]

ALIOSHA [*pleadingly*]. Mama! Mama!

MRS. OSHINSKY [*shaking him*]. I'll mama you, you little devil!

MRS. ROMANOFF [*furiously*]. Take your hands off him! Take your hands off him!

MRS. OSHINSKY. Not until he gets what's coming to him. [*She raises her hand to strike the boy, but he slips out of her grasp and takes refuge behind his mother.*]

MRS. ROMANOFF. How dare you raise a hand to my boy, you verdammte—

Mrs. Oshinsky. Your boy's a loafer, that's what he is—a little good-for-nothing bum!

Mrs. Romanoff. Another word and I'll scratch your face!

Romanoff [*soothingly*]. Tcha, tcha! Little mother!

Mrs. Romanoff. Hold your tongue!

Mrs. Oshinsky [*with a sarcastic laugh*]. Gawd! The way she bosses him! You ain't a man—you're a worm!

Mrs. Romanoff. Do you know to whom you are talking? To your emperor—to your ruler! [*To* Romanoff, *who is about to interrupt.*] Keep your mouth shut!

Mrs. Oshinsky [*with a snort of contempt*]. Ruler! He's a hell of a ruler, he is! He can't even rule his own wife.

Romanoff [*before his wife can reply*]. There is but one Ruler. [*He points his finger upward. The women are visibly subdued.*]

Romanoff [*quietly*]. What has he done, my Aliosha?

Mrs. Oshinsky. What's he done? He's given my Vanka a bloody nose, that's what he's done!

Romanoff. That was wrong, Aliosha!

Aliosha [*protesting*]. But, papa—

Mrs. Oshinsky. There's not a better boy in the Tobolsk than my Vanka. He's a blessed little lamb—

Mrs. Romanoff. Your Vanka is a little sneak, that's what he is! He deserves six bloody noses!

Mrs. Oshinsky [*belligerently*]. If you call my Vanka a sneak, I'll—

Romanoff. No, no! Aliosha was wrong. To strike a fellow creature is to strike God's image. Come, Aliosha, tell Mrs. Oshinsky that you have sinned; ask her forgiveness. [Aliosha *does not answer.*] You see! He is dumb with remorse!

Mrs. Oshinsky. Remorse, me eye! He's an stubborn as a pig. It's no wonder, though, considerin' the Dutch blood that's in him.

Mrs. Romanoff. [*fuming*]. Donnerwetter! Das ist aber ein bischen zu viel!

Romanoff [*hastily interfering*]. No more harsh words! We

all live together in sorrow and sin. What does it profit, then, that we judge one another? The great Judge sees all and understands all. [*Putting his hand on* MRS. OSHINSKY'S *arm.*] Go then, Olga Ivanovna. Aliosha has learned his lesson. Let there be peace between us. Go and may God bless you!

[MRS. OSHINSKY *looks at him, is about to reply, stops and looks at him again.* ROMANOFF *retains his calm, untroubled demeanor.*]

MRS. OSHINSKY [*explosively*]. Aw! You give me a pain. [*She goes out quickly, slamming the door behind her.*]

MRS. ROMANOFF [*bursting out*]. Of course! Make a fool of me! Take her part against me! Your own wife you stand there and make a fool of!

ROMANOFF. Little mother—

MRS. ROMANOFF. Ach! Schon wieder little mother! Immer little mother, little mother! You care much how they insult me—

ROMANOFF [*spreading his hands*]. But, little mother—

MRS. ROMANOFF. Never mind! I heard enough! [*Turning to* ALIOSHA.] Why do you fight in the streets like a peasant? Is that how you were brought up?

ALIOSHA. But, mama, the boys—

MRS. ROMANOFF. De boys! De boys! Fifty times already I told you, you shouldn't play with those boys. But you don't listen.

ALIOSHA [*tearfully*]. But, mama, it's no fun playing alone. In the Winter Palace, I never had anybody to play with and I used to be so lonesome. And now, when there are boys to play with, you won't let me. [*He bursts out crying.*]

MRS. ROMANOFF [*melting*]. Ach! Mein armes Kind. [*She takes him in her arms.*] You shall play with anybody you like. [*Sharply.*] Look at your face! Were you playing in a pig-pen? Und your stockings! There was not a hole in them this morning! Do you think I got nothing to do but darn?

ALIOSHA. I couldn't help it, mama!

MRS. ROMANOFF. Couldn't help it! Vy do you fight?

ROMANOFF [*gravely*]. Fighting is wrong, Aliosha. Come here to papa. [ALIOSHA *goes to him and sits on his knee.*] Why did you fight with Vanka?

ALIOSHA. I'll tell you all about it, papa. We were playing revolution—

ROMANOFF. Revolution?

ALIOSHA. Yes. We always play revolution. Jaakov is always Kerensky because he's the biggest and he can lick any of us.

ROMANOFF. But Kerensky is not big.

ALIOSHA. I know. But everybody wants to be Kerensky and if we didn't let Jaakov, he'd lick us.

MRS. ROMANOFF [*indignantly*]. The bully.

ALIOSHA. And I always have to be you, papa.

MRS. ROMANOFF [*brightening*]. You see! Even the boys recognize the born ruler!

ROMANOFF [*with more understanding*]. And how do you play your game?

ALIOSHA. First they make me adjucate.

ROMANOFF [*quietly*]. Abdicate, Aliosha.

ALIOSHA [*doubtfully*]. The boys all say adjucate.

ROMANOFF. And then?

ALIOSHA. Then if I have any money, they take it away from me.

MRS. ROMANOFF [*angrily*]. They steal your money?

ALIOSHA. It's not stealing. [*Importantly*]. It's confiscating the crown property. Then they lock me in the cellar—we make believe the cellar is Tsarskoe-Selo—and they give me bread and water.

MRS. ROMANOFF. It is impossible! They dare not do such things!

ROMANOFF [*stroking the boy's head*]. And it is always you they lock in the cellar?

ALIOSHA. Yes. They never let me play anything but Czar. I told them it isn't fair. I told them it's not my fault that you're my papa, but they—

ROMANOFF [*covering his face with his hands*]. My poor Aliosha.

MRS. ROMANOFF [*sharply*]. Dummkopf! You have made your papa cry!

ALIOSHA [*bewildered*]. But, papa, I didn't mean to! [*Pleading.*] Papa, papa, forgive me! [*He bursts into tears.*]

ROMANOFF [*soothing him*]. No, no! It is nothing! It is nothing, Aliosha! And now—and now tell me why you fought with Vanka.

ALIOSHA. Because when I was in the cellar today, waiting for them to let me out, Vanka came in—he had run away from the others—and he said if I gave him three kopecks, he'd start a counter-revolution. So I punched him in the nose—the little sneak!

MRS. ROMANOFF [*greatly troubled*]. Ach Gott!

ROMANOFF [*kissing the boy's forehead, his eyes glistening with tears of joy*]. Ah! Aliosha! Aliosha! [*Gravely.*] But fighting is wrong. Do you know what our great Tolstoi says, Aliosha? He says—

MRS. ROMANOFF [*irritably*]. Is this a time to talk Tolstoi?

ROMANOFF [*submissively*]. Mama is right! After supper we will talk. Go now, Aliosha, and—and wash your face.

ALIOSHA. Yes, papa. [*He goes toward the kitchen.*]

MRS. ROMANOFF. Not in the kitchen. Go in the bedroom! And don't come till I call you!

ALIOSHA. Yes, mama. [*He goes out at the upper door.*]

ROMANOFF [*shaking his head, tenderly*]. Little Aliosha! [*He looks after him, dreamily.*]

MRS. ROMANOFF. Sit down, Nicky, and pay attention to what I have to say.

ROMANOFF [*meekly*]. Yes, little mother. [*He seats himself on the chair on which* BERNSTORFF *has left his books.*]

ROMANOFF [*rising, in surprise*]. Hello! Books! [*He picks them up.* MRS. ROMANOFF *utters an exclamation.*]

ROMANOFF [*examining the titles in amazement*]. Liebknecht! Harden! [*Gazing at his wife, incredulously.*] Little mother, have you—?

MRS. ROMANOFF [*in despair*]. Ach, it is no use! He should speak for himself. [*She goes to the door of the kitchen.*] Come in, please!

[ROMANOFF *looks at her in amazement.* BERNSTORFF *enters.*]

ROMANOFF [*in bewilderment*]. Von Bernstorff! Johann!

BERNSTORFF [*making profound obeisance*]. Your majesty!

ROMANOFF. No, no! Johann! I am Nicholas Romanoff, a Russian citizen.

BERNSTORFF [*protesting*]. I cannot permit your majesty—

ROMANOFF. Not majesty! Romanoff, Johann! Or Nicholas!

BERNSTORFF. I would not presume—

ROMANOFF. Presume! It is not presumption to call a man by his name! It is—it is courtesy. But sit down.

[*They seat themselves. There is an embarrassed silence.*]

ROMANOFF [*suddenly*]. Is this the vision of which you spoke, little mother?

MRS. ROMANOFF [*shortly*]. Yes.

BERNSTORFF [*in astonishment*]. I beg your pardon!

ROMANOFF. It is nothing. Well, Johann, I am glad to see you again. It is many years since we met. We did not think then, that our next meeting would be in Siberia—like this!

BERNSTORFF [*with just the right inflection*]. Alas! We did not!

ROMANOFF. No. We seemed secure in our high places then— you and I. We did not dream that we would be shorn of our power—

BERNSTORFF [*expostulating*]. But—!

ROMANOFF. But there is One above—One who knows all. One who watches and waits. [*Changing his tone.*] But I am glad, Johann, that you have turned to me in your hour of exile—

BERNSTORFF. This is—[*Turning to* MRS. ROMANOFF.] Has not your majesty explained—?

MRS. ROMANOFF. I have explained nothing.

ROMANOFF [*smiling*]. It does not need an explanation. I am not a child. I understand everything. These books—they are yours, are they not?

BERNSTORFF. Yes, but—

ROMANOFF [*with a self-satisfied smile*]. Aha! Just as I thought. The books betray your secret, Johann. [*Holding up the books.*] Liebknecht, Harden! You have caught the fever! And they have exiled you! Well, what else could you expect?

BERNSTORFF [*with a show of irritation*]. Your majesty has entirely misapprehended the situation—if you will pardon me for presuming to say so. These books are merely—merely what our enemies are so fond of calling camouflage.

ROMANOFF. Camouflage? What is camouflage?

BERNSTORFF. It is the science of making a thing appear to be something which it is not.

ROMANOFF [*enlightened*]. Ah! You mean diplomacy!

BERNSTORFF. No, your majesty. Diplomacy is not a science; it is a fine art, the chief principle of which is that while a straight line may be the shortest distance between two points, no true artist ever draws a straight line. But these are abstractions in which, as a practical man, I take but little interest. What concerns me now is to impress upon your majesty that far from being an object of imperial disfavor, I come here an honored emissary of my emperor, entrusted with a diplomatic mission of the utmost importance.

ROMANOFF [*amazed*]. You come to Siberia on a diplomatic mission!

BERNSTORFF [*nodding*]. Yes, your majesty. A mission of extreme delicacy which I cannot help believing has been placed in my hands in recognition of my amazing success in America. My imperial master—

ROMANOFF [*interrupting, interested*]. Tell me, how is Willy?

BERNSTORFF [*solemnly*]. The All-Highest is enjoying his usual imperial ill-health.

ROMANOFF [*nodding sympathetically*]. I know. It's in the blood. [*Confidentially.*] Too much intermarriage, Johann. It's not good. Gobloff—[*Explanatorily.*]—he's the foreman of my gang—Gobloff was telling me only yesterday about a cousin of his who married her uncle—

BERNSTORFF. Sire!

MRS. ROMANOFF. Ach, Nicky! How you talk!

ROMANOFF [*looking from one to the other*]. What have I said?

BERNSTORFF. Your majesty must forgive me, but I cannot remain passive while my emperor is likened to a—a member of the laboring classes.

ROMANOFF. Come, come, Johann! Don't be too hard on Willy. We mustn't find fault with him because he is not a workman. It is the fault of his education. [*He goes on placidly, ignoring* BERNSTORFF'S *apoplectic attempt to interrupt.*] Look at me! You know what I was five years ago—a year ago, for that matter. I had no appetite, I could not sleep, I had a cough. And now! Ask the little mother how I eat! And when I get into my bed at night, not even a bomb could wake me up. As for my health—[*He rises, walks to* BERNSTORFF *and doubles his arm.*] Feel that!

BERNSTORFF [*stiffly*]. I would not presume!

ROMANOFF. Nonsense. It is only a man's soul that is sacred. Feel!

BERNSTORFF [*feeling the arm gingerly; with conventional politeness*]. Superb!

ROMANOFF [*resuming his seat*]. A year ago it was as soft as a stewed rabbit! Hard work, Johann. That is the secret of happiness and the secret of health! Do you know what is the most beautiful sight in the world? A snow-bank disappearing under your shovel! [*Gravely.*] If it doesn't snow to-morrow, there'll be no work the next day. It seems to me the winters are growing milder. Have you noticed it, Johann?

BERNSTORFF [*with unconscious grimness*]. Not in Germany.

ROMANOFF. Well, perhaps not. Perhaps it only seems so because I am outdoors, instead of in the Winter Palace.

MRS. ROMANOFF [*shaking her head; half aloud*]. It is hopeless!

ROMANOFF. What is hopeless?

BERNSTORFF [*hastily*]. Your majesty, if you will permit me to explain—

ROMANOFF [*absorbed in his own thoughts*]. Johann, has Willy ever thought of going to work?

BERNSTORFF [*drawing himself up*]. I must ask your majesty—

ROMANOFF. It might be the making of him, Johann. He is not without his qualities. [*Thoughtfully.*] And yet—and yet, he would not make a good workman. He is too much the dilettante. He has never taken anything seriously—except himself. To the good workman, the work is everything, himself nothing.

BERNSTORFF [*with drawn lips*]. Your majesty, I can no longer delay acquainting you with the object of my visit. [*Slowly and impressively.*] I have come to restore your majesty to his imperial throne.

[ROMANOFF *gives him a scared look and then bursts into uproarious laughter.*]

ROMANOFF [*the tears streaming down his cheeks*]. Hear him! Hear him, little mother! They have made a jester of him in America! [*He notices that the others are grave and silent.*] You do not laugh, little mother?

MRS. ROMANOFF [*in a choking voice*]. It is no laughing matter.

ROMANOFF [*sobered*]. No laughing matter?

BERNSTORFF [*significantly*]. I am in earnest, your majesty!

ROMANOFF [*becoming frightened*]. In earnest?

BERNSTORFF. Yes, your majesty.

ROMANOFF [*crossing himself*]. Holy Father! He has gone mad!

BERNSTORFF [*volubly*]. Everything is arranged. I, myself, have been in Petrograd and have personally examined every detail of the machinery which will accomplish our purpose. The plan is simplicity itself. A week from today all the members of the Provisional Government will meet in the Duma Building. At a given signal, the building will be blown up, three regiments of picked German troops, disguised as Cossacks and armed with machine-guns, will clear the streets, your majesty will address from a balcony a selected gathering which will hail you with wild enthusiasm, six newspapers which we have purchased will announce the restoration, a million pounds of bread will be distributed to the populace, two or three thousand of the more ardent revolutonists will be publicly executed, as an indication of your majesty's firmness. There will be—

ROMANOFF. Enough! These are the evil dreams of a degenerate!

BERNSTORFF [*haughtily*]. They are the carefully formulated plans of the German Foreign Office.

ROMANOFF [*raising his voice*]. That is the same—[*He stops and covers his eyes with his hands, then continues sadly, without a trace of anger.*] You are living in a dead age, Johann. You are talking of things that are no more—of things that happened when Nicholas Second was Czar of Russia. [*He bows his head sadly.*]

MRS. ROMANOFF [*with a cry of sympathy*]. Nicky! [*She takes his hand.*]

BERNSTORFF [*misunderstanding him*]. Do not be disheartened your majesty! You have but to place yourself entirely in my hands and within the week you will again be Nicholas Second, Czar of Russia.

ROMANOFF [*slowly*]. Johann, tell me, why have you come to me?

BERNSTORFF [*pityingly*]. Perhaps I have not made myself clear. [*He speaks slowly and deliberately.*] I have come to restore—

ROMANOFF. Forgive me, if I am stupid. I am not a diplomat and these things are not easy for me to understand. But you will be patient with me. Tell me, then; you wish—that is to say, Willy wishes—that there should be an emperor in Russia?

BERNSTORFF [*beginning to explain*]. Certainly; we wish to restore—

ROMANOFF [*raising his hand*]. You wish an emperor. And all the means whereby an emperor may be obtained are in readiness?

BERNSTORFF. Everything! I assure your majesty you need have no fear—

ROMANOFF [*as before*]. Yes, yes! I do not doubt it! What I

wish to know is why you come to me—to me, Nicholas Romanoff, Russian citizen, residing in Tobolsk?

BERNSTORFF [*in utter astonishment*]. To whom else should we come?

ROMANOFF. Are there not millions of other workmen in Russia? Why do you not go to them? Or better still, why do you not make yourself emperor? You have all the necessary qualities. I have none.

BERNSTORFF [*with the pitying patience which one displays towards the very old, the very young and the weak in intellect*]. Your majesty is the ranking member of the ruling family of Russia and—

ROMANOFF. I am Nicholas Romanoff, member of the International Union of Snow-Shovellers and Junk-Dealers, Local No. 27. [*Suddenly.*] Even if I wanted to, it would be impossible for me to accept. [*He fishes in his pocket, produces a little book and hurriedly turns the pages.*] Here is it! By-law number eleven. "Unless endorsed by two-thirds of the members, no member of the union shall be permitted to hold a political office of any kind." [*He hands the book triumphantly to* BERNSTORFF, *who puts it down with a suppressed exclamation of disgust.*]

MRS. ROMANOFF [*impatiently*]. Vell, suppose they did put you out of the union?

ROMANOFF. What! when I have just paid a year's dues in advance. Ten rubles is not to be sneezed at! And, above all, to betray the union! No, no! You had better go elsewhere, Johann.

BERNSTORFF [*beginning to let his impatience show*]. It is impossible! There is no one but your majesty who can lay claim to the title! It is your divine right!

ROMANOFF [*solemnly*]. Don't be blasphemous, Johann.

BERNSTORFF [*staggered*]. Blasphemous!

ROMANOFF. You must be careful how you speak of God. To me God is God, and not a clerk in the German Foreign Office. Do you think that if God chose kings, he would have chosen me—or Willy? You might as well call God a fool outright.

MRS. ROMANOFF [*shocked*]. Ach, Nicky.

BERNSTORFF. I cannot pretend to enjoy your majesty's pleasantries—

ROMANOFF. Ah, Johann, to the Philistine, the truth is always a pleasantry. [*As* BERNSTORFF *is about to speak.*] Say no more. Let us talk of something else—of cooking or gardening.

BERNSTORFF [*bursting out*]. Does your majesty not understand that I am offering him an opportunity to return to Petrograd? An opportunity that will never come again?

ROMANOFF. And why should I return to Petrograd?

BERNSTORFF. Surely you do not wish always to live here.

ROMANOFF. Why not? In Petrograd I was only an emperor, here I am a man.

BERNSTORFF. It is unbelievable! No man, with such an alternative, would choose to live in exile!

ROMANOFF [*with a sad laugh*]. Exile! [*He rises deliberately, walks to the window and raises the shade.*] Come here, Johann!

BERNSTORFF [*trembling*]. Your majesty would not betray me!

ROMANOFF [*with his first touch of bitterness*]. Betray you! No, you are safe here! This is not Wilhelmstrasse! [*In his usual tones.*] I wish but to show you something.

[BERNSTORFF *hesitates, then goes to the window.* MRS. ROMANOFF *covers her eyes.*]

ROMANOFF [*taking* BERNSTORFF's *arm*]. Look there, beyond the church. Do you see that great wooden building, that looks like a monstrous coffin?

BERNSTROFF. That barracks, you mean?

ROMANOFF. Yes, that barracks. Do you know what it was used for, that barracks—in the days when Nicholas Second was Czar of all the Russias? It was there they housed the exiles —the Siberian exiles, the exiles on their way to the mines, the exiles on their way to torture, to starvation, to death. Two hundred thousand exiles have warped those boards with their tears—two hundred thousand in the reign of Nicholas Second, last of the Romanoff dynasty. Two hundred thousand!

And now I am here—an exile! And I cannot look out of my window without seeing that barracks. Johann! [*He draws* BERNSTORFF *away from the window and points solemnly upwards. There is an impressive silence.*]

BERNSTORFF [*fighting down everything resembling sentimentality*]. Your majesty is not the last of the Romanoffs!

ROMANOFF. What do you say?

BERNSTORFF. I say that you may speak for yourself, but you cannot speak for your heir—for the Grand Duke Alexis! You cannot throw away his empire.

ROMANOFF [*troubled*]. Aliosha!

MRS. ROMANOFF [*roused*]. Yes, Nicky! It is his birthright. Grigory said he was born to rule. For his sake, Nicholas, we must go back.

ROMANOFF. For his sake! He is happy here!

BERNSTORFF. He is a child.

ROMANOFF [*passionately*]. And do you think I was never a child! [*With sudden determination.*] He shall speak for himself.

MRS. ROMANOFF [*alarmed*]. What are you going to do?

ROMANOFF. He shall decide. [*He calls into the bedroom.*] Aliosha!

ALIOSHA'S VOICE. Yes, papa!

BERNSTORFF. It is folly!

ROMANOFF [*solemnly*]. All men are fools in the sight of God! [ALIOSHA *enters and stops short at seeing a stranger.*]

BERNSTORFF [*kissing his hand*]. Your royal highness!

ALIOSHA [*shrinking from him*]. Papa, why does everyone mock me?

ROMANOFF [*in a voice trembling with emotion*]. Aliosha, this gentleman wishes to know whether you—

BERNSTORFF [*interrupting*]. I wish to know whether you want to become Czar of all the Russias?
[ALIOSHA *looks at him, his lip trembling.*]

ROMANOFF. Answer, Aliosha.

ALIOSHA [*reproachfully*]. You said I could become a horse-doctor!

BERNSTORFF [*desperately*]. I will restore you to your royal station—to your beautiful palace in Petrograd—

ALIOSHA [*with a cry of fright*]. No! Don't make me go back to the Winter Palace! Mama! Mama! Don't let him take me back to the Winter Palace! [*Sobbing hysterically, he buries his face in his mother's lap.*]

MRS. ROMANOFF. No, no, mein liebchen! You shall stay here! You shall not go to the Winter Palace! [*She comforts him.*]

ROMANOFF [*extending his hand*]. Goodbye, Johann! [BERNSTORFF *without a word goes towards the kitchen.*] Not that way! This way!

BERNSTORFF [*stiffly*]. My disguise—

ROMANOFF. You do not need a disguise. You are safe! [*Slyly.*] Perhaps if you tell them who you are, they will make sure that you get safely across the frontier.

BERNSTORFF [*at the door*]. If your majesty should reconsider—
    [ROMANOFF *stops him with a gesture.*]

ROMANOFF [*taking his hand*]. Goodbye, Johann! A safe journey—and pleasanter thoughts! Take a fraternal greeting from Nicholas Romanoff to Wilhelm Hohenzollern. Tell him that when the day comes—not the Day of which he dreamt—but the day that will come—he will find here in Tobolsk food and shelter and a wooden shovel. [*Detaining* BERNSTORFF, *who is fidgeting angrily.*] Tell him that empires rise and empires fall, kings are born and kings die—but in Siberia there is always snow! [*Instinctively he glances towards the window.*] Aha! [*He releases* BERNSTORFF'S *hand and goes to the window.*] Look at it! Fine, big flakes! That means business! [*He stands there oblivious of everything but the falling snow.* BERNSTROFF *throws him a look, half of pity, half of envy and goes out as the curtain falls.*]

THE LATE CAPTAIN CROW

A Comic Tragedy of the Spanish Main

BY

LOUISE VAN VOORHIS ARMSTRONG

LOUISE VAN VOORHIS ARMSTRONG

Louise Van Voorhis Armstrong was born in Chicago and spent most of her childhood in Evanston, Illinois. She studied at The Art Institute of Chicago and The University of Michigan, where she took her M.A. degree in 1910. Her interest was divided between art work and writing, but she now devotes most of her time to writing. Married in 1911. Her husband, Harry W. Armstrong, is a Chicago artist. The past seven years she and her husband have spent about half the year at their summer home in Manistee, Michigan, and the winter months in Chicago. She has had much experience as a director of amateur groups, such as The Chicago Art Institute Alumni Players, The Chicago College Club Players, the dramatic department of Northwestern University Settlement of Chicago, and other club and school groups. In 1927 she was the state winner in both Illinois and Michigan in The National Full-Length Play Writing Contest, conducted by The Drama League of America and Longmans, Green & Company. In 1928 she had a few months' work with Professor George Pierce Baker at Yale. About a dozen of her one act plays and pantomimes and two of her long plays have had many productions by Little Theatre and amateur groups throughout the country.

Published Plays: *Dolls; The Doctor of Lonesome Folk; The Old History Book; The Mouse; The Gold Altar; The Waning Moon; Good Roads;* and *The Late Captain Crow.*

CHARACTERS

(In order of appearance)

RALPH GLASBY, *a wounded pirate.*

THOMAS HAWS, *a lean, dark, vicious pirate.*

JACK LURCH, *a gentleman pirate.*

A SPANISH CAPTIVE.

SCARFACE CROW, *Captain of the pirate ship.*

ROGER PYE, *a small, philosophical pirate.*

ENOCH RIDDLE, *a grizzled old sea-dog.*

DAVE CRISP, *a young pirate.*

SCENE: *The cabin of a pirate ship at anchor in the harbor of a captured town in the Spanish Provinces.*

PERIOD: *The early seventeen hundreds.*

TIME: *Late evening.*

ALL RIGHTS RESERVED

The Late Captain Crow is copyright, 1929, by Louise Van V. Armstrong, and 1929, by Samuel French, and is subject to a royalty. All acting rights, professional and amateur, broadcasting by radio, public reading, recitation, etc., are reserved in the United States of America, the British Empire, including the Dominion of Canada, and other countries of the Copyright Union, by the owner. Performance forbidden and right of presentation reserved. Application for the right of performing this play must be made to Samuel French, 25 West 45th St., New York City, N. Y.

THE LATE CAPTAIN CROW

SCENE: *The cabin of a pirate ship at anchor in the harbor of a captured town in the Spanish Provinces. Late evening. A lighted lantern, hung on the wall down right, casts a yellowish light about the room, which is empty, and merges into the moonlight that is sifting in through three windows up center back. The center window is open. Down right is a passage which leads on deck. No door to it is visible. It is a small entry way between two staterooms. Above this, up right, is a door leading into GLASBY'S stateroom. The back wall curves down stage as it joins the left wall. This is the stern of the ship. Well down left is a door, hinged on the up stage side and opening inwards to the Captain's stateroom. It is now open, and a faint glow, as of candle light or a dim lantern, comes from within. A heavy, crudely built wooden table about eight feet long occupies the center of the room. Two high backed chairs and some benches and stools stand near it. A huge jug of rum, bottles, mugs, goblets, a scattered deck of playing cards and two candlesticks with the candles unlighted, are placed at random on the table.*

The door of the stateroom up right opens and RALPH GLASBY, *the mate, enters. He is a big, raw-boned, sandy fellow, and is wounded. His head is tied up with a bandage and his right arm is in a sling. He wears sea breeches, a ragged, stained shirt, and a sash with a knife stuck through it. He moves slowly and painfully and seems a bit dazed at first. He goes to the door down left and peers into the stateroom. He withdraws, closing the door, crosses to the passage down right, and looks off.*

GLASBY. On deck there! Watch! [*He pauses. No answer.*]

Where's the watch? [*No answer.*] Watch, I say! Damn you! [*Still no answer.*] Below there! [*A longer pause. Still no answer.*] Gone! Blast 'em! [*He goes out down right, returning immediately with a lighted lantern. He lights the candles with it, and then hangs it on a hook in the wall near the door down left. He goes to the table, pours out a mug of rum and sits drinking, feeling of his injured head from time to time. Voices are heard through the open window. He listens and rises.*]

VOICE OFF BACK. Ahoy! On board!

GLASBY [*approaching the window*]. What boat's that?

HAWS' VOICE. Haws and Lurch.

GLASBY. Come aboard! [*He returns to the table and pours out another drink. Noises off right as the others come aboard.*]

HAWS' VOICE. Over with you! [*Sound of the hatch cover lifted.*] Into the hold with him! [*Sound of a scuffle.*] Down with you! [*The crash of the hatch cover closing.*] Rot there! You rat! [*As he approaches the passage down right.*] Who's on board?

GLASBY. Me, Glasby.

[*Enter* HAWS *and* LURCH. HAWS *is a tall, dark, lean, vicious looking man about thirty. He wears a ragged shirt and sea breeches and has a knife in his sash.* LURCH *is a handsome, young rake, a gentleman pirate, who has taken to the high seas as a quick road to wealth. He wears his shabby finery with a gallant swagger and has a brace of handsome pistols in his belt.*]

LURCH. Where are the others?

GLASBY. Gone! Every blasted soul of 'em! Not even the watch on board! I just come to myself.

LURCH. Well, what can you expect? The Captain's losing his control of them—of course.

GLASBY. Aye! He's losing his grip, Scarface is! So full of rum he's rotting away like a water-logged old hulk ready to sink at her moorings.

HAWS [*bitterly—every word has a poisoned sting*]. We sail at midnight!

GLASBY. The hell! [*He starts to rise hastily in his surprise, winces with pain, and sits down again, nursing his head.*] What for?

LURCH [*mockingly*]. Orders—from Captain Scarface Crow.

GLASBY. Where is he?

HAWS. Down on the wharf—bellowing drunk as usual!

GLASBY. Did anybody get that lowlive Spaniard that smashed my head?

HAWS. I did. He tripped over you and I knifed him as he fell.

GLASBY. Scarface can't mean to sail tonight. We ain't looted the town.

LURCH. Oh, that's all been done! You've been asleep you know.

HAWS. Aye! And the loot divided—what there was of it!

GLASBY. What! [*He again starts up, clutches his head and sinks back.*] Divided! When?

HAWS. At sunset. On the beach. It's all on board now.

GLASBY. Hell! And me not there!

HAWS. Oh, you wasn't forgotten!

LURCH. No. Your share was set aside.

GLASBY. How much?

LURCH. Seventy pieces-of-eight.

GLASBY [*furious.*] You call that my share—

HAWS. It's more than the rest of us got.

LURCH. Yes. You got ten extra as mate, and ten more for being wounded, according to The Articles. The rest of us poor devils got a mere fifty apiece. I'm new on board. I suppose I shouldn't talk. But if this is piracy—Gad! I can do better in the gaming houses at home.

GLASBY. There must have been more than that.

LURCH. Well, that's all we found—

HAWS. So far! That town ain't half sacked!

LURCH. Oh, I suppose there's more all right, but we couldn't find it. The Cabildo was empty as a quill and the soldiers in the fort say they haven't been paid. What little gold we did get came from the warehouses along the wharf—and a little more from the church.

GLASBY. Who looted the church?

LURCH. The Captain—

GLASBY [*instantly suspicious*]. Scarface himself—

HAWS. Oh, we was with him! Anytime I let Scarface loot a church by himself! I was right on his heels every move—Lurch here too.

GLASBY. And there wasn't nothing—

LURCH. A little coin in the box for the poor.

GLASBY. Nothing else?

HAWS. Not another damn thing but a dead priest. He was laying at the foot of some stone stairs going down to the wine cellar with his head stove in.

GLASBY. Who killed him?

HAWS. Nobody. Just fell down stairs and cracked his head open I guess. Then we found a little rat of a Spaniard hid in an empty cask among the wine jars.

LURCH. A carpenter. We brought him with us just now. I suppose the Captain thought we could use him.

GLASBY. Aye. We need a carpenter. Any other prisoners?

LURCH. A few, but just the riff-raff of the town. They wouldn't have any money.

HAWS. Scarface had 'em brought in to him one by one to be questioned. I wasn't there, but he said he didn't get nothing out of 'em, so he locked 'em all up in the jail—all but this carpenter.

GLASBY. What did you do with him?

HAWS. Down in the hold.

[LURCH *rises, stretches, and begins walking about the cabin. He is obviously discontented. The other two sit glowering at the table.*]

LURCH. And so, after acquiring a magnificent fortune of fifty pieces-of-eight, and having a merry hell of a debauch, we shall now set sail at midnight. What do you think of it all, friend Glasby?

GLASBY. Scarface is just a damn fool,

LURCH. A sentiment in which Haws and I heartily agree. What are we going to do about it?

GLASBY. What do the rest of the crew think?

LURCH. Most of them are past thinking, but the few who can, feel as we do.

GLASBY. Riddle too?

HAWS. Riddle don't say much. He's been with Scarface a long time.

LURCH. Yes. But the old man has sense. The point is—what can we do?

HAWS. If we stay we can scour the woods and get more captives. Hold them for ransom. I know there's gold to be had, and by God, if I was in the Captain's place, I wouldn't stop till I'd wrung every last peseta out of every cock-eyed Spaniard in the whole blasted town.

LURCH. Ah! If you were in the Captain's place! If you could step into the Captain's boots, Haws, perhaps—perhaps things might be different.

GLASBY. What about this here carpenter you fetched along? Have you questioned him?

LURCH. What's the use—if we sail at midnight?

GLASBY. Let's have a look at him anyway.

HAWS. Might as well. I'll fetch him. [*He goes out down right.*]

LURCH [*as he disappears*]. It strikes me, Glasby, that Haws has a damn level head.

GLASBY [*without enthusiasm*]. Aye. And a damn sure hand with a knife.

[*Sounds off right—scuffling, the banging of the hatch, and* HAWS' *voice. "You lousy cur! In there! Damn you!" The* CAPTIVE *is kicked in from down right, where he collapses at the feet of the others.*]

THE CAPTIVE. Piedad, señores! Compasion! Misericordia!

HAWS. Stand on your hind legs, you crawling, little scorpion! Let's have a look at you!

[*The* CAPTIVE *staggers to his feet. He is a small, stocky, middle-aged man with a furtive, rat-like face peering out*] *from under his mat of black hair. He is dressed in coarse clothes, like a workman. His hands are bound behind him.*]

THE CAPTIVE. Piedad! Por los dolores de Maria Santisima!

GLASBY. Cease your whimpering! Damn you!

HAWS. Now listen! We come here for gold—mucho oro! Oro! Do you get that?

THE CAPTIVE. Caramba, señor! I have no gold!

GLASBY. So you speak English, eh?

THE CAPTIVE. Si, señor. I have worked with the English in Jamaica.

HAWS. How long have you been in this town?

THE CAPTIVE. Ten years.

HAWS. Then you can damn well tell us all about it. [*Drawing his knife.*] Now! Where's the gold?

THE CAPTIVE. Madre de Dios, señor! I have no gold. I am only a poor carpenter.

GLASBY. Aye! We know that, but there are rich men in the village. Where's the gold hid?

THE CAPTIVE. I do not know. The rich—they—they have fled into the forest with their treasure and their women. I do not know where they have gone.

LURCH. Is there not a secret hiding place in the forest?

THE CAPTIVE. None that I know. There is little gold, señores. Three months it is since the money ship came.

GLASBY. Is there naught else—plate—jewels—

HAWS. No lies, you Spanish dog! [*He whets his knife on the palm of his hand.*]

THE CAPTIVE. Señores— [*He hesitates, his face working. He is undergoing a mental struggle.*]

LURCH. I take it, friend carpenter, that you prefer to go on living?

THE CAPTIVE. Señores, I—I will tell! [HAWS *returns his knife to his belt.*] Señores, there is a—a necklace—

ALL. Ah!

THE CAPTIVE. It is—it is—un tesoro magnifico—a—a grand —a very great, very rich treasure.

HAWS. Where is it?

GLASBY. Go on! Damn you!

LURCH. What kind of a necklace?

THE CAPTIVE. Diamonds, señores! Black diamonds!

ALL. Black diamonds! God!

THE CAPTIVE. Los Diamentes Negros de Maria Santisima— it is called. You would say—The Black Diamonds of the Madonna.

HAWS. Who's got it?

GLASBY. Aye! Where's it kept?

THE CAPTIVE. In the church.

HAWS. The church!

THE CAPTIVE. It is not there now, señores. They would not leave so great a treasure—when you came.

HAWS. Where is it?

THE CAPTIVE. I know, señores. I know where it is. I—I might be able to get it for you if you would set me free.

LURCH. He may be lying. Tell us more of these diamonds, my man. Have you ever seen them?

THE CAPTIVE. Si, señor. Always at mass. They have hung about the neck of the Virgin these many, many years.

LURCH. Where did they come from?

THE CAPTIVE. From far away, señor. They were taken from an Indian King by a great Spaniard—a Conquistador. Then they were called—The Black Diamonds of Coquimbo.

HAWS. The Black Diamonds of Coquimbo! By all the devils! In this mudhole!

GLASBY. Go on!

THE CAPTIVE. It is said that the jewels are—are malditos— cursed, you would say. The Indian priest put a spell upon them when their King was slain, that they might bring death to any man who should possess them. And it is true, señores. At least it was in the old days. He who first brought them had no sooner returned, when he was bitten by a poisonous snake in his own garden and died in agony. Then the jewels went to his younger brother, and in less than three months he was knifed in the back by a woman as he lay sleeping.

HAWS. Any man might be bitten by a snake or knifed by a wench. 'Tis much the same. What of the jewels?

GLASBY. How came they in the church?

THE CAPTIVE. Because of the curse, señores. The wife of the seventh man who died from having them, feared even to touch them. The priests said if they were given to the Blessed Virgin the curse would be removed, and so it was done. They say that even the priest who carried them to the church was taken soon after with a sunstroke, but now —now they have rested on the white bosom of the Holy Mother so many years that surely they must have been purified, and no curse could remain in them.

HAWS. No more babbling of curses, fool! What of the jewels?

LURCH. Yes. What are they like? You say you have seen them?

THE CAPTIVE. Si, señor. These many years at mass I could never take my eyes from them. [*He seems to gloat over them in memory.*] They are so beautiful—so beautiful—like deep pools at night—like—like the soul of night itself, and the light of the candles twinkled in them like stars. Recently I have worked in the church making repairs—and I have—I have seen the necklace closer.

LURCH. What of the jewels? Go on!

THE CAPTIVE. There are twenty great diamonds. Each one would bring a fortune, señores. They are set in gold and pearls. One time, when the padre was not looking, I even touched the stones with my hand.

HAWS. Where are they? That's what we want to know.

THE CAPTIVE. When you fell upon the town a priest came and took them away.

HAWS. Where is he?

THE CAPTIVE. The priest no longer has the jewels, señor. Another man is keeping them. That I know.

HAWS. What man?

THE CAPTIVE. A man—a man I hate, señor. An enemy of mine.

HAWS. Who is he?

THE CAPTIVE. A—a stranger, señor, who has come to the town but lately.

HAWS. Where is he now?

THE CAPTIVE. I do not know. [*In a sudden, desperate effort.*] Señores, if you will set me free, and give me a knife and one of your small boats, I will go back to the village and kill that man and bring you the black diamonds.

GLASBY. Oh! So you're handy with a knife, eh?

THE CAPTIVE. Señor, even the most peaceful man does not hesitate to kill a dangerous animal.

HAWS. So you think we'd trust you, do you? You sneaking, little viper!

THE CAPTIVE. Señores, I can get you those diamonds. I swear it!

HAWS. We might take him back and let him find this—enemy. What do you say, Lurch?

THE CAPTIVE [*in a panic as* HAWS *mentions going with him*]. No! No, señores! Not that! Not with you! I must go alone! If I do not go alone, I cannot get the jewels!

GLASBY. Lies! The whole damn yarn!

HAWS. Best knife him! [*Draws his knife.*] Still I've heard of The Black Diamonds of Coquimbo.

GLASBY. He's heard tell of 'em too no doubt. It's just lies!

THE CAPTIVE [*throwing himself on his knees before* LURCH]. Piedad, señor! I tell the truth!

LURCH. Might be something to it. Keep him a while.

HAWS. Not long till midnight. Best go if we're going.

VOICE OFF BACK. Ahoy on board! [HAWS *dashes to the window up back.*]

HAWS. What boat's that?

RIDDLE'S VOICE. Captain's dinghy!

HAWS. Come aboard! [*Wheeling around to the others.*] Saints and devils! It's Scarface himself—with Riddle and Pye!

[*At the mention of the* CAPTAIN, *the* CAPTIVE *huddles against the wall to right, trembling with fright.*]

GLASBY. The hell!

PYE'S VOICE. Ahoy on board! Give ush a hand!

HAWS. Aye! Aye, sir! On deck, Lurch!

GLASBY [*indicating the* CAPTIVE]. What about him?

HAWS. Back in the hold—

LURCH [*at the passage down right*]. Too late!

GLASBY [*indicating his own stateroom*]. In there!

[HAWS *kicks the* CAPTIVE *into the stateroom up right and closes the door, as* LURCH *dashes out down right.*]

HAWS. Not a word about them diamonds!

GLASBY. God! No!

HAWS. If he ever got 'em—

GLASBY. When Scarface gets to hell he'll cheat the devil out of brimstone!

[*Confusion and noise off right and the bellowing voice of the* CAPTAIN. *"Rum! Fetch the rum!" Murmur of other voices. "Bring me rum! You rogues!"* CAPTAIN SCARFACE CROW *enters from down right, leaning heavily on* RIDDLE *and* PYE, *who try to steer him across to the stateroom down left.* LURCH *follows them.* CROW *is a tall, gaunt, powerfully built man between forty and fifty, with a cruel, eagle-like face under shaggy, black hair. A diagonal scar, like a cutlass slash, cuts across his face from one temple to his heavy jaw. He wears an elaborate, velvet coat, a handsome garment once, but now ruined, sea breeches, big boots with flaring tops, a sash through which are stuck two flint-lock pistols, and a colored handkerchief tied about his head. His face is ashy white, ghastly in contrast to his black hair and heavy brows, and his eyes have a blank, glassy stare. It is plain that he is not only fearfully drunk, but a very sick man besides.* RIDDLE *is a typical, grizzled old sea-dog, with a keen, hard-boiled, but not unkindly face. He wears a dark coat, sea breeches and has a flint-lock pistol stuck through his belt.* PYE *is a comical, little, blear-eyed derelict, decked out in tawdry finery and a battered cocked hat. He also has a flint-lock pistol.* RIDDLE *is sober.* PYE *is amiably and philosophically drunk, but in no such state as* CROW.]

RIDDLE [*as they enter*]. I wouldn't drink no more tonight, Cap'n.

[CROW *breaks away from them and staggers towards the table. He draws himself up to his full height with a mighty effort, his glazed eyes fixed in a blank stare, and speaks, each word thunderous and distinct.*]

CROW. Scarface Crow wants rum! [*He lurches into a chair and collapses in a heap, his head on the table. The others regard him in disgust.*]

RIDDLE. Come on now, Cap'n. Your bunk's right here. Best sleep it off.

PYE. Good night'sh resht! Make a new man of you! Make a new man of everybody!

[PYE *is bending over him just as* CROW *rouses himself with a roar.*]

CROW. Rum! Ye chattering baboons!

[PYE *reels back, hastily reaches for the rum jug and unsteadily fills a mug.* CROW *grabs it and drains it.* PYE *fills a mug for himself and is about to raise it, when* CROW *grabs it out of his hand and drains it also.*]

PYE [*in disgust*]. Pretty mannersh!

CROW [*somewhat revived*]. On deck, ye dogs! Sail! Sail tonight! Orders! Cap'n Scarface Crow! [*No one makes a move.*] What! Ye stand there—ye swabs—

RIDDLE. Cap'n, mebbe I hadn't ought to say nothin', but I figures we ain't in no condition to sail tonight.

CROW. We sail tonight! Blast ye all! Where's the crew?

HAWS. Back on shore—wallowing in the mud where you left 'em!

RIDDLE. Aye! Haws is right. You can't never get them cutthroats to sail tonight, Cap'n. You'll have a mutiny on your hands.

CROW. Mutiny, by God! You speak to me of mutiny! I'll shoot 'em down! Shoot 'em like dogs! Shoot all of ye down like dogs! Scarface Crow can shoot straight! [*Pulls his flint-lock.*] Does any man here doubt it?

PYE [*nervously.*] Not for a shecond, Cap'n.

RIDDLE. Mebbe it ain't gone so far as mutiny yet, Cap'n, but you can't drag them men on board. Half of 'em you'd have to hoist over the side like so much ballast, and the rest ain't satisfied—

HAWS. None of us is satisfied!

PYE. Not by a damn shight! [*He starts to pound his fist on the table, but misses it.*]

GLASBY. I ain't had no chance on shore at all. It ain't fair!

CROW. You'll get your share of the loot, you whining crocodile!

GLASBY [*in disgust*]. A handful of pieces-of-eight! Do you call that loot?

CROW. It's all you'll get! Damn you! All any of you get! On deck, I say! Or you'll take it to hell with you! Sail tonight! Orders! Cap'n Scarface Crow! All hands on board!

RIDDLE. What's your hurry, Cap'n? There ain't a sail in sight. If you wait till tomorrow we might drag in a few more captives or something—

LURCH. Captain, I'm a new man on board. Perhaps I ought not to say anything, but I think there's more loot in that town.

CROW. Go think in hell! You sea-goin' cock-sparrow!

HAWS [*in a sudden outburst*]. We know there's more! And so do you! [*He is nervously clutching his knife.*]

CROW. You lie! Damn your soul! You fool! Do you look to find diamonds in a dung-hill?

HAWS [*wheeling on him suddenly, his knife half drawn*]. Aye! Black diamonds—perhaps!

[CROW *reels to his feet, grabbing out both pistols. He backs towards the door of the stateroom down left.*]

CROW. On deck, you squirming rattle-snake, afore I blow your brains out! [HAWS *makes a lunge for him.* LURCH *and* GLASBY *grab* HAWS. CROW *has backed, staggering, to the door of the stateroom.*] On deck! You knaves! You scoundrels! You gutter-rats! You black-hearted sons of the devil! On deck, I say! Or God strike me dead, I'll send you all headlong to hell! And Scarface Crow can shoot straight! [*He lurches through the door and slams it. A heavy thud is heard.*]

PYE [*towards the door.*] Pleashant dreamshs!

LURCH. A bit peevish, isn't he?

PYE. He'sh losht hish temper—tha's what he'sh done. Alwaysh loshes hish temper when he'sh in hish cupsh! Getsh abushive!

HAWS [*tensely*]. I could have knifed him! I could have knifed him, I tell you! I got a notion to now! [*He starts towards the door, but* LURCH *restrains him.*]

RIDDLE. Aw, set down, Haws! Set down!

HAWS [*bitterly, as he sits down*]. I could of knifed him—

RIDDLE. Hell! I could have knifed Scarface God knows how many times—but you can't go knifing every man you want to. It's agin' discipline.

LURCH [*thoughtfully*]. Diamonds in dunghill! What put diamonds into his head?

HAWS. Aye! That's what I'd like to know.

RIDDLE. Oh, we hauled in a couple of Indians after you left. They told some fancy yarn about black diamonds.

PYE. Black Diamondsh of the Madonna! Tha'sh what they said.

RIDDLE. Aye! In the church. Don't seem likely. That ain't much of a church.

LURCH [*excitedly to* HAWS]. The same thing—

HAWS. Then it's true!

RIDDLE. Why? Did you hear tell of 'em too?

HAWS. Aye! That carpenter we fetched on board. Him we found in the church!

RIDDLE. Might be, I suppose.

GLASBY. Sure sounds like it.

HAWS. The Black Diamonds of the Madonna! It has a juicy sound, mates!

PYE. Point ish—who'sh got 'em?

HAWS. Aye! That's it.

LURCH. This carpenter claims he knows.

HAWS. Mates! I'll desert afore I'll sail tonight! I'm going back on shore. If there's black diamonds—

LURCH. I'm with you, Haws. I move we all go and take this carpenter along.

GLASBY. Me too!

PYE. Gen'lemen! Le'sh all go!

RIDDLE. Aye! But suppose the rest do come aboard, and Scarface comes to and sails. Then where are we? A handful of us out there in the swamp with all them Spaniards and Indians!

GLASBY. There's something in that.

LURCH. But will the crew come back on board?

RIDDLE. Some of 'em will. Enough mebbe.

LURCH. Will they obey that swine?

RIDDLE. Scarface is handy with a gun. They'll obey if they don't have no other leader perhaps. When there's mutiny, there's got to be a leader.

LURCH. Then I'm for mutiny! And I say again what I said a while ago. I'd like to see Haws here step into the Captain's boots and lead us on to victory! We've had enough of that drunken lout! Haws is fearless—we all know that! He's energetic! He'd make a great Captain! What do you say, gentlemen?

GLASBY. Haws couldn't do no worse than Scarface—

PYE. An'—an' he'd do it a damn shight quicker!

RIDDLE. Well, I ain't got nothin' agin' you, Haws, if you want to be Cap'n—so long as you don't go knifing anybody that's useful. If you must knife somebody, go pick a nigger —or somebody we don't need. But don't forget, mates, while we're doin' all this talking, Scarface is in there and liable to come to.

[PYE *tiptoes to the stateroom door and listens.*]

PYE. Quiet ash a moushe!

GLASBY. Aye! What are we going to do with him?

HAWS. What the hell did you bring him back on board for?

RIDDLE. Orders—from Cap'n Scarface Crow.

LURCH. Couldn't you tip him overboard?

HAWS [*jumping up*]. What's to prevent me knifing him now?

RIDDLE. Aw, set down, Haws!

HAWS. Why not get rid of him?

RIDDLE. I ain't got no objection to getting rid of him, but it ain't good discipline. Wouldn't matter if you was to kill him in a fight, but just to go in there and knife him—it—it ain't setting a good example to the crew. Once that kind of thing gets started on board, they ain't satisfied till they've all had a hand at it.

GLASBY. It's a pity some wench didn't knife him on shore.

[LURCH *suddenly becomes very thoughtful.*]

RIDDLE. Aye! If somebody else had done it—somebody that ain't one of the crew—

PYE. It would have been a perfect God-shend!

GLASBY. He ain't no good to nobody now—Scarface ain't.

RIDDLE. I reckon you're right.

LURCH [*bringing his fist down on the table*]. Mates! I have an idea!

HAWS. Well?

LURCH. The carpenter!

GLASBY. What about him?

LURCH. Let's get the carpenter to knife him!

RIDDLE. That mangy, little carpenter! He ain't got the guts!

LURCH. Oh, yes! He asked leave to go back to the village to knife his enemy. Anyway he could be scared into anything.

HAWS. I could just as well do it myself.

LURCH. I know. But if he does it, it can't be blamed on any of us. The Captain wanted to see him. We took him in there and he knifed the Captain. Very simple.

GLASBY. I see. If he done it, none of the rest of us could ever say any of us done it. That ain't no bad idea!

RIDDLE. And what does we do with this here carpenter afterwards?

LURCH. Well—let's see. First, we make him tell us where the diamonds are, or else we go along with him and get them. We tell him if he doesn't produce the jewels, we'll turn him over to the crew and have him hanged from the yard-arm—for killing the Captain.

RIDDLE. Lurch, it's a wonder your brains don't split your head wide open.

LURCH. Well, is there anything wrong with that plan?

HAWS. It suits me.

PYE. Le'sh do it!

GLASBY. I'm in favor.

RIDDLE. I wonder if it's wise. Mebbe so. Scarface, he's on the rocks all right—bound to sink afore long anyway. I wouldn't want to do for him myself—not that I got any objection to losing him—but just as a matter of sentiment—on account of old times and all that. Scarface and me has sailed on many a cruise together. Still, I ain't making any objection.

HAWS. Let's fetch the carpenter.

LURCH. Let me talk to him. [*He goes to the door of the state-room up right, opens it and motions for the man to come out.*] I say, carpenter! A word with you if you please!

[*The* CAPTIVE *edges out of the door. He is even more nervous than before and there is now a sort of frenzy in his rat-like face. He winces as they all swing around towards him.*]

LURCH [*after a pause*]. Now that you have had time for thought, my man, I take it that you still wish to go on living?

THE CAPTIVE [*from his soul*]. Si, señor!

LURCH. Of course. You're a sensible man. Life is sweet. There are pretty women in your town—and good rum, if our Captain has left any. Well, there is something you can do for us, carpenter, and if you do it—and do it well—

THE CAPTIVE. The diamonds, señor—

LURCH. Yes, the diamonds later. But there is a little favor we want you to do for us first.

THE CAPTIVE. Si, señor.

LURCH. You spoke of wanting to knife an enemy of yours. [THE CAPTIVE *starts.*] I take it it wouldn't be your first experience in killing a man?

THE CAPTIVE. Perhaps not, señor, but I am a peaceful—

LURCH. Of course. You're a peaceful, law abiding citizen, like ourselves, but sometimes the most tranquil men in the world find it necessary to kill an enemy.

THE CAPTIVE. Si, señor.

LURCH. Exactly. Now there is a man in there—[*Indicating the stateroom down left.*]—who is an enemy of ours—

THE CAPTIVE. El Capitán!

HAWS. How did you know it was the Captain?

THE CAPTIVE. I am right there, señor. [*Indicating the stateroom up right.*] I am not deaf and your Capitán roars like a bull.

LURCH. He does indeed. At present he is lying there in a drunken stupor. He is perfectly harmless, but we think it better for him never to awaken. You are to go in there and kill him. After that you will get us the diamonds and we will set you free. We might even consider letting you have one of the diamonds. How about it, carpenter?

THE CAPTIVE [*throwing back his head—a fanatical gleam in his eyes*]. Por Dios, señores! I will!

ALL. Good!

LURCH. Cut the ropes!

GLASBY. Keep him covered!

[PYE, RIDDLE *and* LURCH *draw their pistols.* HAWS *cuts the ropes from the* CAPTIVE'S *wrists.* GLASBY *starts to hand him his knife, but* HAWS *brushes him aside and thrusts his own knife into the* CAPTIVE'S *hand.*]

HAWS. Mine, by God! Since I can't do it myself!

[LURCH *hands* HAWS *one of his brace of pistols.*]

RIDDLE. Better get out of range. Scarface Crow can shoot straight!

[*The pirates crowd up against the left wall, out of range of the stateroom door. All keep the* CAPTIVE *covered. The* CAPTIVE *creeps stealthily towards the door. He opens it. He barely steps over the threshold when he utters an ear-splitting shriek. He darts across the cabin as if fleeing from the devil himself, dropping the knife on the way and disappearing through the passage down right.* HAWS, LURCH *and* PYE *dash after him,* HAWS *in the lead. A splash is heard.*]

HAWS' *voice just outside*—"*Jumped overboard!*" RIDDLE *and* GLASBY *have gone to the window up back.* RIDDLE *leans out.*]

RIDDLE. Jumped overboard, eh? By God, he did!

GLASBY. Does the fool think he can swim ashore? There! He's coming up!

[*A shot is heard off right.*]

RIDDLE [*casually*]. Haws got him.

GLASBY. 'Aye. He's done for.

[HAWS, LURCH *and* PYE *return.*]

HAWS. The damn, little stingin' lizard! [*To* LURCH.] That's what you get for being decent to a Spaniard!

LURCH [*with a sudden thought*]. Blood of a pig! Could that scoundrel have had the diamonds on him?

HAWS. He was in the church!

LURCH. That dead priest—

GLASBY. Wouldn't that just be hell now—

RIDDLE. Aw, there ain't no diamonds! It's all lies.

LURCH. Did he kill the Captain?

GLASBY. Couldn't have—that quick.

RIDDLE. No. He was hardly inside the door.

HAWS [*discovering his knife and picking it up*]. No blood on the knife.

LURCH. What made him give that yell?

HAWS. Just a trick, damn his soul! Well, I'll do it myself. Should of in the first place.

RIDDLE. Have it your own way.

GLASBY. Might as well.

LURCH. Be careful. It's funny that yell didn't wake him up.

[HAWS *crosses to the door, knife ready. He opens it and steps inside as the others watch tensely. Instantly he staggers out.*]

HAWS. God and the devil! He's *dead!*

PYE. You done a nice, speedy job, Haws.

HAWS. I didn't kill him!

LURCH. Did the Spaniard?

HAWS. No!

GLASBY. Who done it then?

HAWS. Nobody done it! He's dead, I tell you—just a layin' there—dead!

RIDDLE. Aw, he's just sleepin' it off!

HAWS. Go look, if you don't believe me.

[RIDDLE *and* LURCH *go into the stateroom.* GLASBY *follows towards the door.* PYE *edges away timorously.* HAWS *stands center, clutching the table. For once he is somewhat shaken.*]

LURCH [*coming out*]. He *is* dead!

RIDDLE [*also coming out*]. Aye! He's dead all right.

GLASBY. Old Scarface—dead! If that don't beat hell!

LURCH. So that's what scared the carpenter.

PYE. How—how can he be dead—if—if none of ush done it?

RIDDLE. Rum done it, mates.

GLASBY. Aye! Rum!

HAWS. Don't seem possible. Him in there—dead—and us sitting here—not knowing—

GLASBY. Wonder how long—

RIDDLE. We didn't hear nothin'.

HAWS. When a man gets shot in a fight or knifed in a brawl there ain't nothin' queer about it. That's—that's just natural. You can understand it. But just plain dying—like this—

GLASBY. Aye! Like he was right here— Kinda creepy—I calls it.

PYE. Grim s-s-s-specter of Death! [*He turns slowly around, surveying the cabin with his flint-lock levelled, as if to shoot the specter.*]

LURCH. It is a bit gruesome. Still, you were going to kill him, Haws.

HAWS. I know—but that's different.

GLASBY. Do you suppose the crew'll believe he—just up and died?

RIDDLE. Everybody'll think Haws done it o' course. Well, I reckon we got to bury him as soon as they come on board.

LURCH. Why wait till they come back? Look here, mates! Why not bury him now and say nothing about it when the rest come? Just tell them he isn't here. We can't sail without him of course. Then we can go back to look for him on shore. I'm not ready to give up those diamonds yet.

HAWS. Nor I! We could get hold of them Indians.

GLASBY. Got to bury him anyhow. Might as well be now.

RIDDLE. I suppose it 'ud save a lot of talking—but the crew may be along side by now. Take a look, Haws.

HAWS [going to the window up back]. Nothin' in sight but a canoe with one man aboard—just leaving port. [He pauses.] The tide's going out.

GLASBY. Then Scarface 'ud float out along with it.

RIDDLE. Aye! Kinda too bad. Old Scarface just dying natural. Don't seem like him.

LURCH. Come! Let's go in there.

HAWS. Aye! Best get at it.

[HAWS, LURCH and RIDDLE go into the stateroom down left. GLASBY and PYE stand at the door looking in. The voices of the men inside are heard just beyond the door.]

RIDDLE. Let's get him up on the bunk.

HAWS. Pick up his feet, Lurch.

RIDDLE. Gimme a hand here, Haws. [A pause.]

LURCH. We can wrap him up in the blanket.

RIDDLE. Aye. That'll do.

GLASBY. Take his coat off. I ain't got no good coat now—and I ain't had no chance on shore.

RIDDLE. All right. Lift him up.

LURCH. Here's his pistols.

RIDDLE. Hand 'em out to Pye. We can go over the loot afterwards.

[LURCH hands the pistols out to PYE, who gingerly lays them on a bench.]

LURCH. Better take him out there.

RIDDLE. Aye. We could see better.

HAWS. Clear the table, Pye.

[PYE and GLASBY go to the table and remove the rum, mugs, etc., to the benches. Then each one picks up a candle. They are standing, one at each end of the table, as the other *men come in, carrying the remains of* SCARFACE, *loosely wrapped in a dark blanket. The men deposit their burden on the table.* PYE *solemnly places a candle at his head.* GLASBY *follows suit and places one at his feet.* LURCH *draws back the blanket. The* CAPTAIN'S *coat has been removed. The men crowd around, masking him from the front as he lies in state.*]

GLASBY. Something around his neck.

HAWS [*snatching it*]. The key to his chest!

RIDDLE. Put it over there with his guns. We can divide later.

    [HAWS *reluctantly does so.*]

GLASBY. What did you do with his coat?

LURCH. It's in there.

HAWS [*who has been bending over the body*]. Guess there ain't nothin' more.

RIDDLE. What about his boots? Anybody want them?

PYE. Now's your chance, Haws.

GLASBY. Aye! You can step into the Cap'n's boots now if you like.

HAWS [*with a shudder*]. No dead man's boots for me!

RIDDLE. Might as well wrap him up. Fetch a bit of line, Lurch.

    [LURCH *goes out down right.*]

GLASBY. Seems kinda funny—old Scarface a layin' there dead.

PYE. Might have been one of ush!

GLASBY. Aye.

PYE. Sh-sh-sh-sholemn thought!

    [LURCH *returns with the rope.*]

RIDDLE. He's been a great sea-dog in his day, Scarface has.

GLASBY. Aye! He's scuttled many a ship and sacked many a town. He allus done it thorough too—Scarface did.

LURCH. Well, do we tie him up?

HAWS. Might as well. [*They proceed to do so.*]

RIDDLE. Kinda too bad for an old pirate like him to go like this.

GLASBY. Aye! Just sunk at his moorings.

RIDDLE. He was a credit to the callin' of piracy in his prime.

Seems kind of a pity—just heavin' him over the side without no ceremony nor nothin'.

GLASBY. We ain't got no prayer book.

PYE. No.

RIDDLE. Seems like we'd ought to do somethin'.

PYE. Shomebody might shay a few wordsh.

GLASBY. Guess Riddle's known him the longest.

RIDDLE. I wouldn't know what to say.

GLASBY. Nor me.

HAWS. What's the use of saying anything?

RIDDLE. Ain't much use I guess. Still, if it was one of us—

GLASBY. Aye! If it was one of us seems like we'd kind of expect some sort of services or somethin'. He was Cap'n.

RIDDLE. Aye.

[*All are deadly serious except* LURCH, *who is vastly amused.*]

LURCH. I suggest that Pye say a few words.

PYE. Me?

GLASBY. Well, that might do.

[LURCH *has filled a mug of rum. He gives it to* PYE.]

LURCH. Come on, Pye. Have a drink first.

[PYE *takes a drink and hands the mug back to* LURCH.]

PYE. What am I goin' to shay?

LURCH. Oh, you know. Tell about the deceased.

GLASBY. An'—an' wish him good luck on the voyage. Like they do at a regular funeral.

PYE. Well, here goesh! [*He steps to the middle of the group, standing in front of the table. He is in deadly earnest, as are all the others except* LURCH. *He clears his throat.*] Gen'le-men, we are gathered together in—in s-s-sorrow—to view the remainsh of the late Cap'n Scarface Crow—a man who —a man who—ash all of you know—hash had—a blame-lessh career ash one of the most notorioush pirates of the Spanish Main.—Though of a s-s-somewhat grasping nature in mattersh concerning loot, he wash held in respect by all thoshe of hish calling, an'—an' wash everywhere known as a man of—of almost s-s-s-supernatural intrepidity, drunk or shober. Now that the s-s-sinister shadow of Death hash brought to a closhe the life of this fearlessh shea-dog and buccaneer, mostly on account of rum, which he no doubt regretsh even more than we do ourselves, we—we now—we now conshign hish remainsh to the shea, which hash witneshed sho many of his illustrioush deedsh.— An—an we commend his s-s-soul to everlashting peacsh— [*He stops. This does not sound quite right, but he tries to fix it.*]—to—to everlashting peacsh—which—which we realish ish foreign to hish nature, but we hope he may get ushed to it. In case the c-c-celestial gates ish closed to Cap'n Crow, on account of some that may hold that hish life wash one long s-s-s-succession of s-s-sinful deedsh—it should be borne in mind that hish calling was that of Piracy! Whatever a man attemptsh to do in thish world, he should do to the utmosht limit of hish powersh. An—an—all thoshe who have known the late Cap'n Scarface Crow—will agree that ash a pirate, he wash about ash complete a s-s-success ash anybody could find thish s-s-side of hell—for which he should be given due credit in thish life—and in the life to come! Amen.

[*All relax.*]

RIDDLE. I guess that ought to do.

GLASBY. That ain't so bad. Guess we don't know no hymns to sing.

RIDDLE. Guess not. Well, might as well finish the job. Come on, mates. Give us a hand.

[RIDDLE, HAWS, LURCH and PYE *pick up the body and carry it out through the passage down right.* GLASBY *follows and stands watching until a splash is heard. He then turns, crosses, and goes into the stateroom down left. He comes out with the* CAPTAIN'S *coat just as the others return from down right.*]

HAWS. Here! What are you doing with that coat? We ain't gone through it yet.

GLASBY. I was just fetching it out.

RIDDLE. Might as well go through it now.

[*All crowd around the coat.* LURCH *and* HAWS *go through the pockets as* GLASBY *holds it.*]

HAWS. Ain't a thing here.

[PYE *turns over one of the cuffs of the sleeve. Several playing cards fall out on the floor.*]

GLASBY. Look there! Wouldn't you know!

PYE [*picking up the cards*]. All aches too! [*Starts to put them in his pocket.*]

HAWS. Oh! You're going to use 'em, are you?

PYE. Guessh I found 'em!

HAWS. Well, let's get his chest.

GLASBY. Aye! The chest!

[HAWS *and* LURCH *go into the stateroom down left and return immediately, carrying the chest. They set it down center.*]

LURCH. Here it is.

HAWS. It ain't heavy.

[*All crowd around and* RIDDLE *unlocks it. All bend over it.*]

RIDDLE. Ain't much here.

LURCH. A little silver.

HAWS. Damn little!

LURCH [*holding up a small bag*]. There's coin in this.

HAWS. Just his share of this raid I guess. Pour it out.

[LURCH *does so. The sound of coins falling in the chest is heard.*]

GLASBY. Aye. Just silver. How much did he take?

HAWS. Double share. A hundred pieces-of-eight.

RIDDLE. Twenty apiece for us.

LURCH. Shall we divide it now?

RIDDLE. Best wait. The rest might come.

HAWS. Aye! Best take it back in there I guess.

[RIDDLE *locks it and* LURCH *and* HAWS *take it back to the stateroom, returning immediately.*]

PYE. Le'sh all have a drink!

GLASBY. Aye! Rum!